REFLECTIONS
DURING
COVID-19
2020

Queen Mother
Dr. Delois Blakely

REFLECTIONS DURING CORONAVIRUS 2020

Copyright ©2021 by Queen Mother Dr. Delois Blakely

All rights reserved. No part of this book may be reproduced, copied, stored or transmitted in any form or by any means – graphic, electronic, or mechanical, including photocopying, recording, or information storage and retrieval systems without the prior written permission of Queen Mother Dr. Delois Blakely or HOV Publishing except where permitted by law.

HOV Publishing a division of HOV, LLC.
www.hovpub.com
hopeofvision@gmail.com

Cover Design: Hope of Vision Designs
Editor/Proofread: Dianna Knox-Cooper / Jacquelene Barnes

Contact the Author, Queen Mother Dr. Delois Blakely at:
blakelynews@gmail.com

For further information regarding special discounts on bulk purchases, please contact blakelynews@gmail.com

ISBN Paperback: 978-1-942871-93-4

10 9 8 7 6 5 4 3 2 1

Printed in the United States of America

Acknowledgements

I, Queen Mother Dr. Delois Blakely, would like to acknowledge all persons that practiced social distancing during the Coronavirus pandemic as I prayed and fasted in reflection of God's Omnipotence as The Creator of all things from March 2020 to September 2020.

Every step of the way, the HIGH HOLY DAYS of different religions crossed my path. I reflected on the Judaic Passover (Wednesday, April 8th, 2020 – Thursday, April 16th, 2020), the Christian Eastertide (Sunday, April 12, 2020 – Sunday, May 31st, 2020) and the Islamic Ramadan (Thursday, April 23rd, 2020 – Saturday, May 23rd, 2020) and other holy days from different religions and spiritualities.

This body of work '**REFLECTIONS**' represents '**A HEALING MODALITY**'.

This period of time took me back to my childhood with overwhelming impact filled with the spirit and love of God.

I would like to acknowledge Sister Zakiyyah in the presence of Muhammad as she prays to God Allah. Evangelist Janis Prince holds to God's unchanging hands as she embraced me in that spirit.

I prayed from 3:00am to 6:00am every morning as I called "The Early Morning Risers" to hear my reflections. "The Early Morning Risers" and other listeners in search of our Supreme Maker and Redeemer: Captain Matar Diop Kane, Harvey Dupiton, Jacint "Cindy" Campbell, Rev. Leslie Miles, Dr. Janis C. Brooks, Sheila Collins, Bassirou Sambe, Mama Moses-Mary Moore, Mocha Brown, Mr. Don Levy, Mama Gail Clouden, Mama Asantewaa Harris, Dr. S. Bowland, Mrs. Mary Green-Cohen Winston, Kim Poole, Patricia Muhammad,

Dr. Joseph Hickman, Mychal Jefferson, Mr. Kenneth Stevens, Carolyn Jenkins, Louis David, Sharonne Salaam, Nitin Kumar Vaid, Patricia L. Bradley, Dior Fall, Agnes Dey, James Russell Branch, Guiyi Tiffany Zhou, John John Semi, Chairman Hershel Daniels, Min. Ashe Kujenga, Edward "Teddy" Hall, George Green, Natalia Maria Tomassini, Mustapha Jatta, Ebou Saine, Mustapha Sowe, Mohamed Fofanah, Patreinnah Acosta-Pelle, Mr. Leslie Sapp, Jophia Nanker Gupar, Angela Sayles, Ibrahima Diallo, Guy Djoken, John Oko Nyaku, Jimbes Hardy, Rev. Adeyemi Adedeji, Shiying Hao, Atty Diane Eubanks, Dr Arlene Spann, Zufan Tesfai, Juanita Pierre-Louis, Donna Tsufura, Dr Jacqueline Mohair, Marie Umeh, Cindy Owens, Carolyn Jones, Comfort Dondo, Chantal Gahie, Dandi (Lou) Amanan, Adja Sy, Don Joi, Doris Tipton, Jimmie Lee Blakely, Tracy Green, Dr Angelique Walker-Smith, Abela Aleano Rupia,

Guruji Dileepkumar Thankappan, U.S. Congressman Adriano Espaillat. God spared our lives, we give thanks!

Kenneth Amanze, NFF proofreader of this work is scholarly and brilliant. With a mind that radiates the gift of God, he proofread my work with an analytical and logical process. May God continue to lead and guide him.

NFF Jason Rosario, as the spirit of our ancestors guided him and kept him on the sacred path of life to produce the musical sound of the revelation of God with the beat and the rhythm of eternal life. We ask God to keep Jason on the sacred path of life and bless him as a recording engineer to my audio body of work "REFLECTIONS".

I would like to also thank Harlem Women International/NFF, Global Women Africa Network, Pan African Young women, Dominican Sunday Inc., NFF colleagues and other interfaith groups.

I would like to give special thanks and appreciation to New Future Foundation, Inc. and Fortune Empire for supporting me on this Divine Journey.

This body of work is dedicated to all Corona Virus Victims and their families.

It is also dedicated to Community Minister Abdul Hafeez Muhammad, a Giant of the Fruit of Islam. He transitioned due to Coronavirus. He gave me all the time in the world when we last spoke and greeted each other on 125th Street in Harlem at the street naming for Dr. Yosef Ben-Jochannan, Renowned African Historian.

It is also dedicated to Mayor David Dinkins and his beloved wife of 67 years, Joyce Dinkins, exemplary role models, both have left us during this time of Coronavirus. The Mayor was a gentleman and displayed kindness in Harlem and New York City. He especially showed love towards Queen Mother Audley

Moore and me. May David and Joyce Dinkins always be with us in spirit.

Finally, this body of work is dedicated to Bishop Nathaniel S. Snipes of True Church of God in Harlem, New York. Bishop Snipes, one of our beloved ancestors, left his art which celebrates us with a gift for all to see the reflections of God through the trees of life.

TREE OF LIFE
*By: Bishop Nathaniel S. Snipes,
True Church of God in Harlem, New York*

International Women's Day March 8, 2021

"Women in leadership: Achieving an equal future in a COVID-19 world."

Recognition of the following women: Amina J. Mohammed; Deputy Secretary-General of the United Nations and Chair of the United Nations Sustainable Development Group, Verónica Michelle Bachelet Jeria; High Commissioner of Human Rights, Mary Robinson; Former UN High Commissioner for Human Rights, Anne-Marie Bernadel; Former Assistant to the UN High Commissioner for Human Rights, Phumzile Mlambo-Ngcuka; United Nations Under-Secretary-General and Executive Director of UN Women (pictured below with Queen Mother), Honorable Gertrude Mongella; Secretary General, Fourth World Conference on Women, Beijing, China; Special Envoy to the Secretary General on Women's Issues and Development, María

Fernanda Espinosa Garcés (Ecuador); Former President of the General Assembly (2018), Daniela Bas; Director, Commission for Social Development, Melissa Fleming; UN Under-Secretary-General for Global Communications, Hawa Maria Diallo; Chief, Civil Society Unit Outreach Division, United Nations Department of Global Communications (DGC), Judyith Duncan; International Hip Hop Conference for Peace (2001), Ruth Brinkley; NFF-DGC Youth Advisor and CSW Representative at the UN, H.E. Cairo Eubanks; NFF Jamaica-DGC Youth Representative, Cristina Duarte; Under-Secretary-General for Africa, Fatima Kyari Mohammed; Permanent Observer for African Union, Arikana Chihombori-quao; Former Ambassador African Union, Washington, D.C., Nana Konadu Agyeman-Rawlings; Former First Lady of Ghana, H.E. Dame Pauline Kedem Tallen; Honorable Minister For Womens Affairs, Nigeria, Secretary Dr. Mrs. Safiya Umar,

Nigeria, Former Ambassador Joy Ogwu, Nigeria, H.E. Elisabeth Moreno; Minister of Gender Equality, France, Ms. Chamathya Fernando and Ms. Anika Jane Dorothy; Representatives of Mexico, Kamala Harris; U.S. Vice-President, Hillary Clinton; Former First Lady and Former U.S. Secretary of State, Madeline Albright; first female U.S. Secretary of State, Kirsten Gillibrand; U.S. Senator and Speaker of the House of Representatives, Nancy Pelosi; U.S. Congresswomen; Karen Bass, Sheila Jackson-Lee, Barbara Lee, Maxine Waters and Yvette Clark. Samia Suluhu Hassan; First woman Head of State of the United Republic of Tanzania, Most Honourable Portia Simpson-Miller; First woman Prime Minister of Jamaica, Sanna Mirella Marin; Prime Minister of Finland, youngest Prime Minister in the EU, Pennelope Beckles; President of the UN Women Executive Board and Permanent Representative of Trinidad and Tobago to the United

Nations, Dr. Ruomei LI; Chair of Women in Power (WIP) Chair of IEEE PES, WIP Liaison in IEEE WIP, China, Queen Esther Ejim and Chief Joyce Adewumi of Nigeria; Traditional African Rulers, Rania Nashar; winner of the Distinguished Arab Woman Award in Economics, Banking (2020). Arab League, all other Member States, Houry Geudelekian; Chair of UN NGO CSW/NY and Susan O'Malley; Former Chair of CSW (2019), Sheila Katzman and Yvonne O'Neal; CSW Members, Attorney. Deadria Farmer-Paellmann; Director of The Restitution Study Group - for their work towards attaining Redress, Reparations and Repatriation, Mrs. Alma Rangel; The First Lady of Harlem; Gloria Steinem; American feminist journalist and social political activist, Countess Esther de Pommery; Swiss Activist, Professor Mandisa Monakali; Founder and Executive Director of Ilitha Labantu, Lauryn Hill; singer, rapper, songwriter, record producer and Queen of Hip Hop, Laverne Brown; former Director of Operation CrossRoads Africa, Terra Renee; Producer, Black Women in Cinema, CSW Women visited Harlem and ate soul food hosted by Pat Stevenson, Publisher/Editor, Harlem Community News, Gail Brewer; Borough President of Manhattan, New York City and Pioneer of Women's Rights, other local officials and grassroots women of the world of Civil Society.

A Special Thanks to all of the United Nations Peace Security Women Officers.

Queen Mother with Phumzile Mlambo-Ngcuka; United Nations Under-Secretary-General and Executive Director of UN Women

Queen Mother with Malala Yousafzai; Pakistani activist for female education and the youngest Nobel Prize laureate

Queen Mother with Asha-Rose Mtengeti Migiro; Former Deputy Secretary General from Tanzania and Amina J. Mohammed; Deputy Secretary-General of the United Nations and Chair of the United Nations Sustainable Development Group

Queen Mother with NGO CSW Women - Dr. Ruomei LI; Chair of Women in Power (WIP) Chair of IEEE PES, WIP Liaison in IEEE WIP, a Board Member and Houry Geudelekian; Chair of UN NGO CSW/NY

Queen Mother Moore & Queen Mother Dr. Blakely

"Reparations – NOW" ~ *Queen Mother Audley Moore*
"Cut The Check" ~ *Queen Mother Dr. Delois Blakely*

Queen Mother Dr. Delois Blakely
Right side of the photo:
Her Excellency Gertrude Ibengwe Mongella
photo taken in The United Republic of Tanzania.

Preface

In this period of time, I thank The Creator, for allowing me to share the inspirations that God gave to me, which has inspired me to go on. During the time that I was set down, March 5th, 2020, it was revealed to me, ***"God runs the world and we run around in it."***

God shut all of us down for a time of inner search and reflection. During the time, I was sanctioned to pray, fast and go through a period of healing with the love of my mother and father in the spiritual realm and with God. This period of time took me back to my childhood it. impacted me, and it was filled with the Spirit and Love of God.

I thank you, my extended family, for rearing me and bringing me up in a way that I will never forget the presence of God in my life.

This body of work, compiled from March through September 2020 (over the High Holy

Period of Easter, Passover and Ramadan, and any other time of high holy spirituality) in search of self, are my reflections during this period of time that I would like to share with the world.

I thank God for allowing me to serve the community for 60 years; 10 years dedicated to Jesus Christ, serving God and God alone in the Convent of the Roman Catholic Church as Sister Noelita Marie, FHM. I was a Humanitarian for 50 years, and a lay person serving the world through the United Nations and traveling the world widely. I continued my dedication and service as a World Wide Chaplain in hospitals, prisons, military bases, communities, villages, parishes, townships, neighborhoods and in the streets. I pray that God will continue to lead and guide me and keep me on the sacred path of life.

Foreword

Profile

I had a quest for God at the age of 9 years old, when I used to sing in the Church, as a child. As I continued to grow, I was in search of serving others in hospitals. After school, between the ages of 14 and 15, I would sing and read the Bible to the sick. I would also make little neighborhood runs such as going to the store for the elders and shut-in. I felt as if I was a part of their extended family. As a youth I enjoyed serving and helping others and my parents never prohibited me from doing so. I shared many stories about my extended family in the neighborhood. Throughout all of my life, it seems that I have had a calling directly from God.

As a young girl I left the Deep South,

Florida, and traveled to New York City. At the age of 16 years old (1958), I entered a Roman Catholic Convent and stayed for 10 years. I made final vows to dedicate my life to Christ as his Bride. I took the vows of poverty, chastity, and obedience to the Order of The Franciscan Handmaids of The Most Pure Heart of Mary.

I lived in the Mother House in Harlem, where Mother Theresa of Calcutta, India, lived for a period of time. Other visiting Roman Catholic Nuns also stayed with us from time to time in the Convent in Harlem, New York, New York.

At the age of 26 years old (1969 to the Present), I founded my own not-for-profit organization, multi-ethnic, multi-cultural, for young people; New Future Foundation, Inc. "With Youth, For Youth, and By Youth" in New York City. I continue to work with youth in education, culture, recreation and innovation. That is the work of New Future Foundation with the assistance of Board Members; Congresswoman Shirley Chisholm, Judge William Booth, David Barry and Dr. Doxey Wilkerson, Mentor; Dr. Angie Brooks, First African woman President of the General Assembly at the United Nations. Supported by New York University, Yeshivah University, New York Mission Society, New York City Board of Education, New York Chamber of Commerce and Industry and a host of other not-for-profit and Private Sector Organizations. At the United Nations with Non-Government Organizations (NGO) Accreditation with the Economic and Social Council (ECOSOC) and the Department of Global Communications (DGC) status. One of the greatest experiences in my life was witnessing with the naked eye, the NASA launching and landing of the space shuttle at the Kennedy Space Center, I was invited by my God-Brother, Astronaut Ronald McNair (1984). I was Dame in Honor and

Merit of the Sovereign Order of the Hospitallers of Saint John of Jerusalem Knights of Malta (1976). I became the Community Mayor of Harlem (1995 to Present).

I was enstooled as a Queen Mother in Amapondo, Volta Region in Ghana (1995). I was received by the King of the Ashanti Kingdom, Otumfuo Osei Tutu II, and sent to his mother, Nana Afia Kobi Serwaa Ampem II (the oldest Queen Mother, now an Ancestor), to be blessed and instructed in my duties as Queen Mother in North America (Harlem, NY) representing the African Descendants and the Diaspora (1995-Present). I assisted Queen Mother Audley Moore for 20 years. I carry her legacy in the passing of Queen Mother Moore, who lived almost 100 years (1898 - 1997). She was known as the Mother of the Reparations Movement. Among her many admirers were Winnie Madikizela-Mandela; South African anti-apartheid activist and freedom fighter and

Alpharita Constantia (Rita) Marley; Cuban-born Jamaican singer and Revolutionary Musician with her husband, Bob Marley. Dr. Jean Bennett and Maxine Mantano adored and assisted Queen Mother Moore. In the 1980s, Queen Mother Moore and I shared many unique cultural and traditional experiences in Africa such as Maasai Land and in the Caribbean such as Nyabinghi Temple in Jamaica. A highlight of Queen Mother's life; I introduced Queen Mother Moore on the record in addressing the Heads of State of Africa of the OAU, Chaired by Former President of The Republic of Zambia, Kenneth Kaunda in Addis Ababa, Ethiopia (1987). She was also elated and honored to have been in attendance at the Million Man March, in the company of Rosa Parks and Dr. Dorothy Height. I spoke on Queen Mother Moore's behalf as she sat in her wheelchair on the National Mall in Washington D.C. The March was called by Minister Louis Farrakhan, of the

Nation of Islam (1995). I participated in international affairs by escorting Sister Winnie Mandela to the Million Woman March in Philadephia, PA, which was led by Sis. Empress Phile' Chionesu (Empress Chi); Originator & CEO (1997). I was Presiding Elder at the Million Youth March in Harlem led by Khalid Muhammad (1998).

I graduated from the Franciscan Handmaids of The Most Pure Heart of Mary College, affiliated with The Catholic University of America, (1965) with a Bachelor of Science Degree in Religious Studies. I was a Community Fellow (special) graduate student (1981-82) at the Massachusetts Institute of technology (MIT), an Education Policy Fellow (1982-83) of the International Education Leadership (IEL), a Fulbright Scholar and Ethnographic Researcher in Tanzania; conducted research under President Julius Nyerere, Education for Self-Reliance and Nigeria; accepted at University of Ibadan

(1984-85). I received two Master of Education Degrees, from Harvard University (1982) and Teachers College, Columbia University (1983) and a Doctor of Education Degree from Teachers College (1990). I attended the School of Social Work, School of Business and School of Law at Columbia University (1985-1990). I received scholarships at Peabody Conservatory of Music, Harkness Ballet and Barbizon School of Modeling (1968-1980). I enjoy singing, dancing swimming, biking, fashion and traveling the world. I published scholarly and popular books and articles on self-reliance, education, recreation and culture. Queen Mother enjoys co-directing and co-producing; New Future Foundation Documentary Film by film student of NYU, Sundance - Sister Act for Real trailer and Cannes - Queen Mother Documentary trailer, so far. I accompanied The Middle Passage Monument to its final resting place in the Atlantic Ocean (1999).

Queen Mother led the wagon carrying the remains of the African Ancestors from Wall Street to their final resting place in the historical African Burial Grounds, New York City (2003). I received the Mother Theresa of Calcutta Award (2011). I was appointed as Queen Mother of Hip Hop by KRS1, Kool Herc and recognized by The Zulu Nation (2014). Artist, Pawel Althamer, created a monument entitled 'Queen Mother of Reality' inspired by me and dedicated to the work of social justice against homelessness (2014). At the 50th Selma Bridge Crossing Jubilee, I was blessed to receive an Honorary Foot Soldier Medallion. Attorney (Fire) Rose Sanders and Political Prisoner & Environmental Justice Activist, Connie Tucker were lead organizers for the Jubilee, Jessica Barker and Rev. Brenda Ward were also on the team (2015). At the 2015 NGO Conference in Support of the Seventieth (70th) Anniversary of the United Nations, I was one of four honored in the General Assembly (GA) Hall. My phrase "Civil Society", meaning "inclusion of all" is now part of the UN vernacular. After the dedication of the Ark of Return at the United Nations by Secretary General Ban Ki-moon, Jamaica and other Member States; my DNA test which was administered on Juneteenth at the Ark, revealed that I Am a true African; North, South, East, West and Central, an African of the Continent (2015). Jerold Hickiggerbar, Prime Minister of the American Slave Nation presented Queen Mother with their flag and title of Ambassador during the Fifteenth (15) Session of the Indigenous People's Forum at the United Nations Church Center (2016). From the Federation of World Peace and Love (FOWPAL) I received a Lifetime Achievement Award (2018). I was surprised with the International Inspiring Woman Award at the Ilitha Labantu 30th Anniversary Gala Dinner held in South Africa. Reflection: Call on the Ancestors and the Most High God to STOP ALL FORMS OF VIOLENCE AGAINST WOMEN as I looked upon one of the wonders of the world, The Table Mountain, Cape Town, South Africa (2019).

I received Congress of the United States House of Representatives Proclamation Celebrate and Recognize 50 Years of Humanitarian Service (2019). Received U.S. House of Representatives Proclamation 400 Years of Slavery Trailblazer (2019), received the Congressman Donald M. Payne Sr. Trailblazer Award for Africa 400 Years of Slavery 1619 – 2019 from Nigerian American Public Affairs Committee (NAPAC). Received a Humanitarian Award and United Nations Global Leadership Award from the Trinity International University of Ambassadors (2019). I am a Worldwide Chaplain, Certified by The University of Bethesda Biblical Institute of North America and

OPFP presented by Archbishop Art Rocker (2020). Received the Nelson Mandela International Day Award from UNESCO Peace Center (2020), received Salutations from two U.S. Senators in recognition of receiving the Nelson Mandela Award from UNESCO. Received Outstanding Service to the United Nations and Dedication to the Mission of NFFJ (New Future Foundation Jamaica) from Global Oved Dei Seminary & University (GODSU) (2020); recognized by the World Yoga Community (2020), received the MLK (Martin Luther King) World Peace and Tolerance Lifetime Achievement Award from the African Festival International World Peace Initiative (2021), I was declared a Grandmother of Indigenous People by Authorities of several tribes of Indigenous People of North America, a humbling experience (2021). I have received numerous awards, proclamations, honors, citations and salutations over the years.

As Queen Mother I am engaged from Wall Street to 125th Street in my Royal Court. I have been involved in receiving lines and protocols. I have traveled extensively in Africa and the world to foster friendship, such as Cuba, Russia, China, Libya, South Africa, Israel and a host of other countries. From the 1970s to the Present; I met with many Heads of State of many nations, particularly of African nations in courtesy calls. I addressed the issues of the youth, the poor and powerless. I have a special interest in persons with disabilities. I served at the White House under President Jimmy Carter as a U.S. Honorary Commissioner, alongside Margaret Mead and Mrs. Frances Loeb, for the International Year of the Child (1979). I was a special guest when Pope John Paul 23 spoke at the UN (1979). I was a special guest when Nelson & Winnie Mandela visited, and Nelson Mandela spoke at the United Nations (1990).

In the 1980s and 1990s, I served as Metro-

UNICEF Co-Chair for The Day of the African Child. As UNDP Advisor to the Science and Technology Group; I presented a report about Adaptable and Applied Technology for Africa (2 years) and I was involved with numerous other Boards and Committees. Traveling the world extensively; Queen Mother attended many conferences, meetings and sessions over the years.

High Profile tragedies Queen Mother was involved in; Central Park 5; New York City, framed and persecuted (1989), Foutanga Babani Sissoko; from Mali, framed and persecuted (1995), Amadou Diallo; from Guinea West Africa, 41 shots in New York (1999), Ousmane Zango; from Burkina Faso, killed in warehouse by police (2003), Soumare and Mougassa Families; from Mali West Africa, 10 died (9 children and 1 mother) house fire in the Bronx, NY (2007), Trayvon Martin; Florida, harassed and killed by civilian (2012).

As a member of the World Conference of Mayors, Queen Mother, on a medical mission, organized a team of doctors, led by Dr. David Nyenje, from May Medical Centre Limited, Kampala in Uganda "The Pearl of the Equator" to employ an Emergency Air Medical Ambulance Service to Harlem-Prespbeterian Hospital, led by Dr. Muriel Petioni, for Kumaru Mugerwa, a baby with severe Macrocephaly (enlarged head). Sadly, the baby transitioned before making the trip. What a miracle it was to wash a child for the last prayer of the night of power.

Queen Mother organized the youth to march from Harlem to The United Nations on the International Day of Peace calling for "Street Peace". Secretary General, Kofi Annan, named Muhammad Ali, Anna Cataldi, Michael Douglas, Jane Goodall, and Elie Wiesel as Messengers of Peace (2003). The CSW Women went to Harlem to help Queen Mother launch Queen Mother Coffee created to help African

Women Farmers build sustainability (2006).

St. Paul Community Baptist Church, led by Rev. Dr. Johnny Youngblood, said a farewell prayer in the spirit of our ancestors, The Maafa, for Queen Mother Blakely and Mama-Moses Mary Moore who went to Goree for three months to support Victor Mooney, and witness from the slave house, his second attempt at The Goree Challenge a solo row from Goree to the Brooklyn Bridge (2009).

I was appointed Ambassador of Goodwill (to FESMAN), World Festival of Black Arts and Culture by President Abdoulaye Wade, Senegal (2009), Historically, I was present when U.S. President Barack Obama and Libyan President Muammar Gaddafi spoke at the United Nations (2009).

Queen Mother Blakely carries the legacy of Mama Africa declared on stage by the youth at Life Celebration of Miriam

Makeba World Festival of Black Arts and Culture (2010).

I participated in the No Justice, No Peace March and Rally (NAN) and the March on Washington for Amadou Diallo and others killed by police. I served as an Elder Advisor to Occupy Wall Street (2011). I marched in early marches in Harlem for Black Lives Matter. I witnessed and observed many high level sessions in the United Nations. In 2018 and 2019 I led a delegation to Washington D.C. to meet with Congressional women and U.S. Foreign Affairs (US Immigration and Homeland Security) to understand the procedures to be granted a visa so that a cross-section of women involved with women's issues in their regions could attend the CSW64 Conference scheduled for March 2020. Historically, I was invited and attended many conventions and inaugurations both Democratic and Republican. I also attended many Governor's State of the State Addresses and Mayor's State of the City Addresses for New York State and New York City, respectively. Remaining bipartisan (as Queen Mother must), I observed both sides of Congress of the Impeachment of Donald Trump in 2019.

In 2019, I began what was to be a three year world celebration of 50 years of service to the United Nations as a Humanitarian.

I witnessed the enstoolment of H.E. Angelique Monet; Royal Family of West Africa representing Africans of the Diaspora at the Cannes Film Festival (2019).

In 2020 COVID-19 shut me down (actually all of us). I remained in prayers, fasting and reflection.

The Eternal Project of a Lifetime; The Goree Island Project, Senegal. Returning the kidnapped children of African descendants to their Ancestral Home through the gateway of Mother Africa (2063 and beyond). Proclaimed "Queen Mother of the Trans-Atlantic Slave Trade".

MY MESSAGE TO THE YOUTH; I encourage you to follow my example; go on and live your life to the fullness as The Divine One would have you to do. Be a positive force to be reckoned with as you stay on your sacred path of life.

Touba the holy land of miracles!

Blessing, Blessing, Blessing,

Delois Blakely, 2nd

Queen Mother Dr. Delois Blakely
Community Mayor of Harlem
Ambassador of Goodwill to Africa
Founder/CEO of New Future Foundation Inc.

Contents

God Runs the World	1
God Clothe Me	2
Joy of God	3
God Has It All	5
Be Still	6
Magnificent	7
Holy	8
What's In My Hands	9
Thy Healer	10
Not A One	12
Awesome God	14
Mother's Prayer	15
Earth Is Mine	17
COVID-19	18
Hold Me Father	20
Spirit of God	21
A Rose	22
God's Goodness	23
Power of God	24
Father Blessings	25
Use Me	26
Amazing Grace	28
Miracle Working of God	29
In the Name of Allah	30
Cry For My Mother	32
My God	34
Quiet	35

In This Space	37
Full Moon	39
Duality	41
Revival with Ancestors	43
Black Is Beautiful	45
Selma – Bloody Sunday	48
Travel The World	51
Prayers (AWOTM National Prayer Book)	
Prayer for Human Rights	53
Prayer for Politics	55
Prayer for the United Nations	57
Reflection Journal	59

God Runs the World
March 5, 2020

God runs the world

And we run around in it

Run Run Run

Run Run Run

Run Run Run

As fast as you can

God runs the world

As we run around in it

We run around in it

Run Run Run

Run Run Run

Run Run Run

As fast as you can

Run Run Run

Run Run Run

Run Run Run

God Runs the world

As we Run around in it

God Runs the world

God Clothe Me
April 30, 2020

Clothe me in my right mind.

Oh God to enjoy life.

God you have the last say so.

So be it.

Let me stay in your conscious of righteousness and goodness.

All is well.

Well with my soul…

Joy of God
May 1, 2020

Joy of God
God the Mystic One
God the Divine One
God the Enlightened One
God the Great One
God the Merciful One
God the Good One
God the Powerful One
Just Your Joy
Just Your Joy
Joy of Being in Your Presence
Thank You for allowing me to enjoy You
Just to enjoy You
No-One else…
I enjoy Your Divine Presence so much in my life
A joy I have never experienced
Thank You for allowing me to enjoy You in this moment of time

God's Joy
Being fulfilled in my life
Let me embrace it
The joy of God
God in all things, my Creator
My Creator
Joy of God

God Has It All
May 2, 2020

Shape and mold me in your Divine image and likeness
Clear me and claim me with a stroke of Your Spirit and Grace
…
…
…
…
…
…
…
…
…
…
Reader, join Queen Mother in your version of completing 'God Has It All'

Be Still
May 3, 2020

Be still and know that You are God and God alone the mover and shaker of my life
Oh, Most High God
As I move and shake in Your everlasting vibrations
Let me hold onto Your unchanging movements that
Have been set for me since the beginning of time
Let me be still and know that You are God
Be still
Be still and know that You are God and God alone

Magnificent
May 4, 2020

Thank You for this day of the rising sun that sustains me in the healing grace of Your radiance
Which spins through the Universe with a speeding energy in the atmosphere
Magnificent One, I thank You for awakening and stimulating the nervous system for the use of my senses and innate gifts
Thank You The Magnificent One for this day

Holy
May 5, 2020

Only You are Holy
Oh God this is not a conversation or a
discussion
Of Your Pure Sacredness that overcomes the
shadow of doubt and distrust
In the world of confusion that appears in
Your Divine Presence of existence
Oh God Your Holiness is Greater than a
state of mind that is bound in faith and belief
Holy is the force Greater than myself
Let Your Holiness enrapture and encapture
me in Your Divine Love
Holy, Holy, Holy
God is Holy
Holy is God

What's In My Hands
May 6, 2020

Can I see?
Can I witness?
What God placed in the palm of my hand?
Eternal Abundance
My Heavenly Father
Who knows all of my needs and wants?
I have the faith of a mustard seed
Believing in You, Holy Spirit
Making a way out of no way for me
What's in my hands?
You the deliverer
The Giver of all things
God You are eternal
Just let me enjoy your Blessings
Tell me
What's in my hands
Allow me to open my hands

Thy Healer
May 7, 2020

Mother Father God
I bow down to You
As I call upon my Ancestors
North, South
East and West
Beckon for You
To heal me
From this wretched and sinful place
That sheds no light
Sheds no light in my frail soul
Oh Creator heal me from the crown of
my head to the bottom of my feet
That controls the spine in the middle of
my back
That balances the alertness of my body
and soul
Well-being is my life force
Heal me away from sickness and death

Set me apart from the emerging sacrifice of day and night
Oh, pass me by oh Merciful Savior
Protect me from all harm and danger
Healer, rescue me
In the bosom of Your healing grace
Oh, Divine Healer of Your healing grace
Open my immune system with Your healing grace
Oh, Divine Healer

Not A One
May 8, 2020

No not a one
Not a one
No not a one
Stay on the sacred path
Hold onto God
No not a one
Not a one will save me
Not a one will defend me
Not a one will care for me
Not a one will acknowledge me
Not a one will understand me
Not a one will nurture me
Not a one will shelter me
Not a one will cry for me
Not a one will embrace me
Not a one will stay with me
No not a one
Only depend on You God
And only You

Oh God hear me
And move me
From no not a one
Not a one
No not a one

Awesome God
May 9, 2020

God is Awesome always to behold
Remember God in all situations, trials
and tribulations
That confronts me
In every waking hour
Lean on the Mighty One
My Lord and Master
Who is called by many names
That is worthy to be praised
From the beginning to the end of my journey
God is Awesome

Mother's Prayer
May 10, 2020

On this glorious Mother's Day
I surrender and renew my commitment
To You Most High God
For the good of my children
First conceived in my womb
And gave birth
A Mother's love is a Mother's pain
I ask You to keep them out of the Lion's mouth
As I fear no evil because you are with them
Every mother's cry is a whisper of mourning
Let my children walk through the shadow of death
And fear no evil
That You God are with them
In a mother's prayer
I submit my children to You
The Holy and Mighty One, with them
Turn my children away in a mother's prayer

As I submit my children to You
So Be It
A man
A Woman

Earth Is Mine
May 11, 2020

Earth is mine says the Lord
And all that roams and dwells within it
I thank You for the sound of the tweeting
bird that holds onto the branches of the tree
Rolling away of the white clouds as the sun
bursts through in the twinkling of an eye
As the cosmos sets ablaze to welcome and
receive me
What a perfect and marvelous creation
I thank You
The Great One for releasing a world that
You created
I will never be able to reach or grab but
to know You are God
I ask You, The Creator to bestow upon me
the peace and joy
To sanctify my soul on this earth
I ask

COVID-19
May 12, 2020
Dedicated to Victims

Death – confront of the unaccountable numbers
As I cry and wail
Filled with grief
Save me from this Coronavirus
That plunged the world in deep sadness
In sadness that spit out anger
That is vicious
Reckless
And wicked
Toward this unexplainable disease
That plagued the Universe
A stench that smells like the bowels of the hallowed ground
Fertilizer covers the dust
Molds into clay that sticks and remains for eternity or forever
Let not this pandemic threaten my fate

As Your will be done
Ashes to ashes
Dust to dust
Remain with me Oh God
My Redeemer
Ashes to ashes
Dust to dust

Hold Me Father
May 13, 2020

Dear Father
I beg you to squeeze me
Squeeze me
As tight, tight, tight as You can
Let my breath leave me
As Your fresh air is pumped into my lungs
In the rhythm of Your heartbeat
That flows oxygen to the brain
For me to see another beautiful and inspiring day
Oh Father, giver of life
Hold me tight
Squeeze me, squeeze me
Tight, tight, tight

Spirit of God
May 14, 2020

Cleanse and purify
My body, mind and soul
As you bathe me in the river of Jordan
Let Your Spirit lead and guide me
As I stay on the sacred path of life
Let nothing separate me from You oh God
You the Spirit that is a mystery
And amazing
Spirit of God…

A Rose
May 15, 2020

A Rose You place in my path
To admire as my eyes glance
Upon the tall-stem that refuses to bend
As the thorns that will Prick me and have no mercy
Stand in a formation of protection
The delicate petals open in sight for me to
See the working of the Creator
In awe as I touch the roses
Red, Yellow, White, Orange, and Lavender
Feels like the Fabric of Silk and Velvet
My fingers discovered or found
in a Rose the presence
Of God in a Rose

God's Goodness
May 16, 2020

The Goodness of God is
Everlasting to behold
During the mist of my trials
And tribulations
God is a trusting friend through it all
God is surely good and merciful
God will never abandoned or Forsake Me
His Goodness will be there in
The time of need when all else will fail or flee
How or why I deserve the goodness to live another moment
To rejoice and be happy
In the presence of God's Goodness

Goodness of God
So it is
So be it

Power of God
May 17, 2020

Speak to me in the voice of
Thunder and Lightning
With the sound or row that causes
A split in the earth of destruction
A mudslide that everything in its way
Will perish from the mountain top
Down to the valley and into the sea
Power that brings me to my knees and
Wait for Your Divine intervention
God will turn me around to worship and
Praise you Oh God only You and
You alone as I stretch my hands
And pray as I cry LORD, LORD
rescue me in Your infinite
Wisdom, will and power

Father Blessings
May 18, 2020

Things may come and go
Even human beings in my life
Only you, Father remains and bring
Me through all situations
Let me remember to say thank you
Stay with me as you continue to
Provide for me
My needs, wants and desires
You are my Father, and I am Your daughter
Fashioned in Your image and likeness
I thank You Father for adorning and caring
for me
Keep me under your guidance so I do not
lose my way
Smile upon Me as a loving Father would do
with His
Blessing, Blessings, Blessings
Dad Will You Bless me?
Bless me

Use Me
May 19, 2020

Almighty God as I cry, I shout with
A running nose that is snotty as I blow everywhere
Why me - Why not me
Choking, changing in swallowing my coughing and swallowing
My saliva through my salty wet tears that stream down my face
Use me for Your divine sake
Please use me for Your Glory and Honor
Use me in the morning as my senses unfolds in the heat
Of the day that burns, darkens me
As I bake in the healing cycle of my complexion
Use me in the blanket of blackness
That covers and hides me in the darkness of the evening
That lay me to rest

Use me in my coming in and going out
Just use me almighty God
Use me

Amazing Grace
May 20, 2020

Amazing grace how sweet it is to engage
In the wonder of God's Grace
Make me be still, silent as
A Lagoon to witness Your amazing grace
In this place
My abode, My home
Let me be still know You are
God and God for all ages
May I ask to hold onto You
Save me-Amazing Grace
How sweet it is
It is Sweet
Amazing Grace

Miracle Working of God
May 21, 2020

The wonder of God,
I sprang up like Daylight
Saving time it as the Day began for me
So bright is the sunlight the eyes barely
Peeped In the distance to see the miracle working of God
His mystery constantly appears in my existence
Oh! Holy-Marvelous one
Show me Your sign of Deliverance
Keep me under Your sensational spall
As I witness in my life Your working miracles

In the Name of Allah
May 22, 2020
Inspired and
Dedicated to Amadou Diallo
and hold up his Mother, Kadiatou Diallo,
with love and compassion.

In the name of Allah the Beneficent,
the merciful
Accept my prayers as I worship You and ask
for forgiveness
Of my sins and Transgressions against You
O –Allah, Holy Spirit allow me to be
Submissive to You will and guidance
Knowing and unknowing
O Allah, You are all wise and everlasting
Perfect is You here and after
Great Judge instruct, strengthen and
enlighten me to do good deeds against
misdeeds
Move Satan from around me, a manifested
enemy
O-Allah give me refuge, hide me in Your
immortality

Let me not go astray, Leave You or abandon You
In my Body, Mind and Soul
In Your spirit O-Allah
You are the Greatest
All praise Due to You
All Praise Due to You
All Praise
Amen

Cry For My Mother
June 6, 2020
Dedicated to George Floyd

Mama, Mama, ma, ma, mommy Mu-dear, mother, where are you?
Can you hear me? I can't breathe!
You are the closest thing to me.
I cry and pray for you to hear me.
Breathing in and out, my last breath
that is being choked and snatched, Robbed, and stolen from me.
Hide me in your womb, which is eternal.
Your womb that sheltered me with love and protection A womb that allowed me to survive and live, a womb that kept, nourished and cared for me, throughout the
natural born days of my life.
Mama, Mama, you know me, where are you?
I need you For God sake I hang in the balance of life or death.
Mama, ma, save me,
I love and honor you.

I can't breathe. Shield and protect me, as I lay in your belly, your divine and sacred womb. Your womb allowing me to flourish and grow. And a hiding place that is my destiny for all eternity.
Oh Mama, Mama, Mama, Ma, Ma,
I can't breathe! I call on you to surrender me in justice and peace.
Oh gentle Savior, save me.
Oh God!......

My God

June 6, 2020
To Ancestors

O-my God, my God, my God
O-my God, O-my God
my God, my God
As I slumber and sleep
Have Mercy on me
O-my God, my God, my God
As I groan and mourn
Have Mercy on Me
O-my God, my God and my All
Have Mercy on me
I am tired, tired, tired
Oh- my god, Oh- my God
Take me, hold me – enrapture me as I am
Oh my God, my God, my God
Have Mercy on me
Oh my God

Quiet
June 13, 2020

Quiet beyond, beyond
O Gentle quiet one speak to me
In the secret of your Ministry,
The Mission that is prepared for me
Thanks be to You, oh Gentle Quiet one
I sat in a place that is quiet
Ask of You again to speak to me
I ask, I seek, I look to find You in a place
that is quiet
In this time of distance far, far away to reach
Reckoned and bounded in a world of
confusion turned upside down
In a time that I wonder in dismay that I feel
Your sweet, glorious and marvelous present
I am in a moment of bliss and to hear
Your quiet
Voice that penetrates me with
the spirit of peace and tranquility

Stay and abide with me
Oh, Gentle Quiet One of the Most High
The ruler and controller of all dominions
Oh, Gentle Quiet One

In This Space
July 1, 2020

In this space
God will you stay with me?
God will you hear me?
God will you listen to me?
In a way that where no other will ever find my sacred space
Only we will dwell in peace and harmony
Only we will meet, communicate and live with each other
In this Sacred space that I hold so dear
God will you dwell with me?
God will you hear me?
God will you listen to me?
God will you keep me?
God will you stay with me?
In this space
In this space that is Holy, Righteous and Just
God will you be with me in this space

To comfort, abide and be with me in this space
In this space above all else
In this space

Full Moon
July 2, 2020

The full moon radiates the beauty
of the light and so bright
Move away and disappear from my sight
as I listen to the sound of music
With the tapping of my feet
To the beat of concerto in G major
Swing of my head in a melancholy mood
that causes me to be in a rhythm of ease
and content
Set me in a tone that can connect me to my
inner soul
In search of the pleasure of You Almighty
God
In Your infinite assembly of the
perfect pitch
Full of joy, happiness
As I witness with the naked eye
Your wonder and splendor
As the full moon spins and turns
For everlasting

In the company of You Maker and My Creator of All times
So Be It, So Be It, So Be It

Duality
July 3, 2020

Oh Lord
In a world that is filled with complexities
That one must accept as a puzzle
In the scheme of things
One will be denounced In escaping
As I trod through the path of existence That I must embrace with a will
to understand Gravity and perplexity await me in the duality that I face daily
That await me and will never end
Oh Great Teacher Show me the learning curve of growth
Good-bad, right- wrong, day-night, in-out, up-down, left-right health- sickness, knowing-ignorance, sufficient-need, strength-weakness, happiness-sadness, yes-no, forward- backward, east- west, north-south, rich-poor, love-hate life-death

Oh God

I Am emerged in the human conditions

Please God detach me from the ways of human beings God, hear my prayer

Shape me, mold me and rid me of duality as I seek and strive for Your perfection

Oh Perfect, Powerful and Mighty One All is well

All is well with my soul

All is well

Revival with Ancestors
July 4, 2020
Laid A Monument Dedicated
To The Ancestors In International Waters

Oh God watch over me
As I renew, rejoice and reconnect
To my ancestors of the middle passage of the
transatlantic ocean of the Slave trade
That left me with the terrific pain of horror,
dismay, terror
And the tragedy that scorned and scarred me
for life
From generation to generation
yet not born
In the midst of the troubled
and raging waters of the ocean
I ask You, The Divine One
To enlighten me
Bless me in the spirit of my ancestors
As I pour libation as a manifestation
Of their trials, tribulations, tolerance,
patience and endurance
Who profess the greatest sacrifice for me

I am inspired and humbled at the ordeals that my ancestors bore in their lives
Oh my God
Let me watch, pray and remain vigilant in the ways of my ancestors
Oh God
Ase, Ase, Ase-o

Black Is Beautiful
July 9, 2020

Dedicated to Father Lawrence E. Lucas
(1933 – 2020).
Roman Catholic Priest, born in Harlem;
Father Lucas
was The Black Conscious of Jesus Christ for over
26 years at Resurrection. Father Lucas was
my neighbor as he served as a Senior Priest at
Our Lady of Lourdes Church.
Cardinal Timothy M. Dolan,
Archbishop of New York, presided over his burial.

Black is Beautiful
Let me ask You, Jesus Christ;
Are You the one black, handsome and beautiful man?
I adored You most of my life?
Since my youth, there was no other
Are You the man who was born in a manger?
In a place called Bethlehem?
As a figure of speech many centuries ago?
The shining star followed You everywhere
Are You the man called Jesus, talked about in The Holy Book, The Bible? Are You the

man so humble and pleasing in God's sight?
That bore no malice or hate in Your heart?
A man with wooly hair, burnt feet, big broad nose, dark brown eyes, high cheekbones, tall in stature, built with a thin frame, the picture of good health?
A man that can climb a steep hill, run on a rugged road as the wind moved You forward, onward and onward? Are You The Christ?
In a distance, are You BLACK, BLACK, JET BLACK?
I depict You Black as Ebony the gem of blackness.
Are You the man I am looking for, thither, here and there?
Appear in a silhouette in a naked desert crossing over in a black sea?
In reality the mineral sea, the sea of life, for living in wellness?
Are You the man, walked in Jerusalem?
Set and ate fish at the Sea of Galilee?
Swam and Baptized in the River of Jordan?
Are You the man died on a cross?
Are You the man that said "Father forgive

me, let this cup pass from me, unless it is Thy will"?

Are You the man handsome, beautiful and black?

Like my earthly father, meek and kind in many ways? Sanctified and Holy?

Oh Jesus, Jesus, Jesus; are You the man born black and beautiful? Beautiful and Black?

Black IS beautiful Ase, Ase, Ase-ooo, Amen

Selma – Bloody Sunday
July 26, 2020

Dedicated to **United States Congressman John Lewis'; Civil Rights Icon**, Last Journey Crossing The Edmund Pettus Bridge. And to Mrs. Amelia Boynton-Robinson (who traveled this journey before him, 2015) and Rosa Parks, Mothers of the Movement. Also dedicated to Claudette Colvin; youth in the movement (15 years old at the time).

I thank you God for guiding my Ancestors, through the most trying and the troubling times of their lives Crossing over the bridge to the other side
They just kept coming, coming and coming Crossing over the bridge to the other side
Almighty God, Foot Soldiers that endured the jumping, growling, snarling and gnawing dogs, galloping/stamping the hooves of the horses
Cowardly men kicking, beating with billy clubs
Whipping with a wet rope braided into a raw lash

That ripped the skin wide open, swelled and bled
Into a sore mark Healed with a lasting scar that will never leave you.
A human being suffering by Yelling and screaming
Running and falling Wailing and crying Save me and
Free me Almighty God From
the bondage that is unjust and unrighteous
As I yearn for a touch of FREEDOM as an agitator and a protester
A Right To Vote For My Race, For My People, For My Tribe
To witness the vision for all
to see it, to hear it,
to taste it, to touch it,
to smell it, to be in it
as we walk across the bridge to the other side
Almighty God Continue to shine your gracious and eternal light upon us
as we cross the bridge to the other side
As we can't give up and we can't give in, for the touch of Your divine and marvelous

FREEDOM as I humble myself.
A People
A Woman
A Man
So Be it

Travel The World
September 22, 2020
(Traveled four countries in Europe during the Coronavirus)

In the month of September
as I prayed in the atmosphere
where the clouds surrounded me
on every side and the moon and sun met
awakened me to greet me as I felt that I was
navigated my movements as a bird in the sky
In the flash of flicking light
in the dark that awakened me –
North, South, East and West
Swirling in the air as I land in Portugal,
France, Monaco and "lo and behold"
in the Alpes of Switzerland.
God allowed me to Commune with Him,
like in no other way that one could imagine,
that brought me peace and tranquility.
Let me stay on the path of life, for all to
witness and reflect on the Sacred and Divine
one.

Prayers

3 Excepts from AWOTM: National Prayer Book
By Dr. Tenaria Drummond-Smith
and 52 Co-Authors

Prayer for Human Rights

Prayer by Queen Mother Dr. DeLois Blakely

We call on You, the Divine force within us to be a just people. Help us to be righteous and just towards each other. God hear our prayer and grant our supplication. We come as children seeking Your mercy and Your Divine intervention. Hear our prayer of loving and being fair towards each other. We know that You are a just God, a God of mercy and love. Oh God forgive us all of our sins and transgressions against you and each other. Let us be like You, reflect the image of You of being just towards each other. And show humility in caring for each other with love and respect. We may be different in religion, culture and traditions; teach us how to be tolerant with each other. We are seeking Your just ways towards each other.

Oh our Creator, we all have a right to food. We have a right to clothing from the elements of life. We have a right to shelter. Oh Lord, You knew us before we were ever known or conceived in our mother's wombs. We pray to You to keep us on the sacred path with a sound and just mind. Rid us of all harm and danger toward each other. Help us to cultivate love toward each other that is just and fair. Be merciful to us in our understanding of life. Help us with the Divine consciousness of human rights. What we want for ourselves, let us want for another. God let us be Your justice, speak of Your justice and fairness. Amen

Prayer for Politics

Prayer by Queen Mother Dr. DeLois Blakely

Oh Lord God, we call on you to help us make decisions that are clear and wise. As we engage with the Politicians who are to be a part of governing our lives, with the leadership of righteousness. As we pray for righteousness oh God, for our leaders, our leaders who will work with us to make us whole in our dealings and peaceful in our society. Sustain us in all our ways. Let us endure in Your Divine mercy and grace. Help us to be mindful of each other as we are living as a community, as neighbors looking out for each other. Give us the leadership of men and women who will seek their guidance from You, the Supreme Leader in all things and at all times. Hear us, Mother/Father who art in Heaven and on earth. We ask You to awaken true leadership in our leaders. What more do we ask of You, that our leaders turn to You and You alone for guidance in every decision they make on our behalf? Oh God, leaders make decisions affecting our lives from birth to death. Oh God hear us, show us Your way as we ask that You lead and guide our lives. Make our leaders righteous in all of their decision-making. Help us to sustain our communities and live in harmony with each other. We thank You for all things. We just want to say "Thank you" for hearing our humble prayer and accepting it. Amen

Prayer for the United Nations

Prayer by Queen Mother Dr. DeLois Blakely

Oh Father God, Mother in our consciousness. The Universe, Force of all life. We come to you this day, this perfect day, in your Divine energy that protects us in Your world, and we ask for Your permission to bow down and worship You. We ask You Creator, the giver of all life to Bless the United Nations. In their deliberations as Member States, we ask that You be a part of their discussion in creating a better world, a world that we could pass on as a legacy to our children. Oh God, we stretch our arms as we look toward the hills where all grace comes from, to embrace us and to love us and to nourish us every day of our lives. We ask of Your Divine guidance and counseling to us. Make us live in Your presence. We came here with nothing, and we will leave here with nothing. Let us find the comfort of peace and tranquility with each other as we live with each other. This is our prayer that we echo to You this day.

Teach us humility. Teach us wisdom and understanding. And above all, teach us caring for each other. We ask that You never leave us or forsake us. We ask for Your healing grace on the world, north, south, east and west. Teach us how to be good stewards in protecting Your world with all its dominions. We acknowledge You oh God; we know that You run the world and we run around in the world. We want to thank You for allowing us to do so. So be it, Amen.

REFLECTION JOURNAL

Photo 'Reflections'
Joan Roth, Internationally Acclaimed Photographer

prayerful righteousness devout –

Photos by Joan Roth   Collage design by Jason Rosario

Reflection Journal

Reflection Journal

Reflection Journal

Reflection Journal

Reflection Journal

Reflection Journal

Reflection Journal

Reflection Journal

Reflection Journal

Reflection Journal

Reflection Journal

Reflection Journal

Reflection Journal

Reflection Journal

Reflection Journal

Reflection Journal

Reflection Journal

Reflection Journal

_____
_____
_____
_____
_____
_____
_____
_____
_____
_____
_____
_____
_____
_____
_____
_____
_____
_____

Reflection Journal

Reflection Journal

Reflection Journal

Reflection Journal

www.ingramcontent.com/pod-product-compliance
Lightning Source LLC
Chambersburg PA
CBHW041325110526
44592CB00021B/2825